HOW YOU CAN BE UNIQUE AND THEREBY GET YOUR DREAM JOB

HOW TO MAKE YOURSELF IRRESISTIBLE TO YOUR FUTURE EMPLOYER

ANTON C. HUBER

Copyright © Anton C. Huber
All Rights Reserved.

ISBN 978-1-63940-843-6

This book has been published with all efforts taken to make the material error-free after the consent of the author. However, the author and the publisher do not assume and hereby disclaim any liability to any party for any loss, damage, or disruption caused by errors or omissions, whether such errors or omissions result from negligence, accident, or any other cause.

While every effort has been made to avoid any mistake or omission, this publication is being sold on the condition and understanding that neither the author nor the publishers or printers would be liable in any manner to any person by reason of any mistake or omission in this publication or for any action taken or omitted to be taken or advice rendered or accepted on the basis of this work. For any defect in printing or binding the publishers will be liable only to replace the defective copy by another copy of this work then available.

Contents

Foreword   v

1. Find Strengths - Define Measures   1
2. Expand Focus   7
3. Define Your Customizable Targeted Offer   12
4. Conclusion   17

Disclaimer   19

Foreword

There are vacancies now that several hundred candidates are applying for. In most cases, only one of these people are chosen. But there are always places where applicants receive a rejection because they were not convincing enough. Either way: The chance for you as `one of the many hundreds` applying to get a place - especially your `dream place` - is very small.

As a recruitment specialist I often see thousands of application documents in a single month. Assuming I work 20 working days in the month and I have a time budget of one to two hours per day for the first orientation of applications, you then expect from me - and also from the majority of my colleagues - to spot countless files by the minute in the initial selection, before deciding which one look to look at more closely.

This concerns only a certain class of places because the submission of applications for most places have long been viewed and answered either by assistants, trainees or temporary staff after a certain grid.

Your cancellation then reads: "After intensive study of your very interesting documents, we have come to the conclusion that other candidates are even more suitable." No one tells you that the study was taken from a temporary help who, at that time, sent several dozen more of such cancellations.

You find it not fair? You're absolutely right, but do not complain about it to me please, but with your legislators, who require a certain number of work efforts by the unemployed and through this way makes sure that the many applicants already made it clear in their motivations letter, that they really `don`t feel like it`. So they steal our time from us to intensely check out the more serious candidates.

Why is it now but that someone survives this screening? The answer is quite simple: they attracted positive attention. Who makes his resume with the resume template XYZ from supplier ABC, gets lost in the crowd. Who designed their documents individually and adapted it to the place and his personality stands out and is considered more accurately many cases.

Another success strategy is the application in the hidden job market. In many cases, it is much more successful if you do not apply for advertised positions, but with firms, where `Your profile fits like the missing jigzaw to the puzzle`, in your initiative letter.

This is the content of this book. Figure out what makes you and your offer for a potential employer attractive, use it to find potential prospects for your profile, and from there to convince them with your "unique" deal. If you perform the consistently, you will see how your chances of success and the number of interview invitations rise dramatically.

Good luck with the job search

Yours,

Anton C. Huber

Sr. Recruiting Specialist

ONE
Find strengths - define measures

What is true in the business world, also applies to the labor market: In order to position the product successfully in the market, you have to first analyze the product impartially. Only then are you able to place it right to emphasize strengths, perhaps to compensate for weaknesses and to identify for opportunities and risks.

That is what we are doing here. Only this time it's not about a new, particularly heat-resistant potholder, but you. You provide your employer a specific power to certain conditions and it is through this power that the conclusion of an employment contract is"rented".

Maybe this view reminds you of a "slave trade" and find such an expression inappropriate or even inhuman. You can see it so readily. But if you give the term "human resources" a closer look, you will notice that I am not alone with this view.

The Four-Field-Matrix

The first step is to analyze the actual situation. In a four-field matrix, first enter the strengths and weaknesses of your personal and professional profile. In the second section, we will look at the possibilities. Here you can work out opportunities and risks (threats) in relation to your environment. This involves issues such as the industry, labor market, competition situation and your own network.

Situation	Positive (+)	Negative (-)
Is	Strengths	Weaknesses
Possibility	Chances	Risks

Draw a four-field matrix and set in the various fields your information. Then if you have the opportunity, discuss the outcome with a friend who can give you to an assessment from the outside.

Try to approach the work as open as possible. Forbid yourself from worrying. It does not matter if you overdo it in the first throw or that some things are not quite perfect. You can also create a version 2, 3, etc., until everything fits. If you've set yourself any limits from the start, you run the risk of overlooking certain issues that might be important.

Strengths

Stellen Sie in dieser Rubrik all Ihre persönlichen und beruflichen Stärken zusammen. Beispiele könnten sein:

Personal strengths:

- Perseverance

- Intelligence
- Learned reader
- Good manners
- Flexible working hours and place of residence
- ...

Professional strengths:

- Expertise in ..., ... and ...
- Network of contacts in industry ...
- Experience in the use of ...
- ...

Weaknesses

There is no point in lying. What your weaknesses here openly. This information is intended only for you. Knowing your weaknesses can help you to determine your second step, which is to make a credible offer for your future employer. It makes little sense to apply for a job as a lifeguard when "fear of water" is one of your greatest weaknesses. Think of what weaknesses are worth working on and what you can leave easily.

Chances

In the area of opportunities you figuratively take out the crystal ball and think about which of your characteristics and skills for you could be particularly advantageous. If you are a computer scientist, a decisive competitive advantage could arise from the mastery of certain programming languages. Likewise, the fact that you are active in a service club for many years and thus have a large international network, can be useful for both your job search as well as for your next employer.

Risks

Risks should be considered just as honest as weaknesses. Often, elements that belong to opportunities can also pose risks. So it can be a big risk if you, as a programmer, mainly dominate hardly used programming languages. On the other hand, this means that there are possibly only a few programmers who actively use the said language or want a corresponding location.

The Eight-Field-Matrix

After the Four-field-Matrix of the actual situation has been worked out, we go on to the Eight-field-Matrix to develop a strategy.

	Chances *	Risks *
Strengths *	Use of strengths to increase opportunities	Use of strengths to reduce risks
Weaknesses *	Overcoming weaknesses in order to seize opportunities	Overcoming weaknesses in order to reduce risks

(* Transfer from the four-field-Matrix)

The results of the actual analysis are entered in the four areas. Based on the average amount of strengths and weaknesses with the opportunities and risks, arise your potential and "work orders". In order to obtain meaningful matrices, it has proven that you should not take too many elements from the previous matrix or possibly setting up multiple templates for multiple combinations.

Use of strengths to increase opportunities

The central question here is how you greatly increase your chances by highlighting your strengths or removing any weaknesses. For example you could have obtained a (written) reference from a person, from whom you mentioned your strengths successfully. Or continue to study, acquire a diploma, publish books on u. V. A.

Use of strengths to reduce risks

Potential employers are keen to reduce their risks in the normal case. Every new employee brings opportunities and potential for conflict. You can help your employer to reduce such risks, which is of interest to them, as long he perceives the risk as well.

In addition, it is also important to reduce your own risk in the job search. If you belong to a professional group, where there is a relatively high unemployment rate, there may be a considerable advantage for you if you own not only the traditional technique, but also additional skills that complement your skills in convincing. So it would be a huge advantage for the aforementioned programmers with outdated programming language if he had experience in the migration of functions from the old programming environment in a new, modern software environment.

Overcoming weaknesses in order to seize opportunities

What steps should you go to ensure that existing weaknesses do not reduce your chances? This may be training, coaching measures or completely different approaches.

Overcoming weaknesses in order to reduce risks

What steps should you take to reduce risks? If one of your risks are that you only talk nonsense in stressful situations such as interviews, then perhaps take coaching, practice simple workouts with friends or join a rhetoric-club such as the toastmaster.

Definition of measures

If you have done the work in the eight-field matrix conscientiously, now some measures would have to be brought to light that it is worth addressing in order to increase your chances on the labor market. Create it a list and prioritize the measures according to their importance (paths that significantly improve your chances) and duration to implement it. Points that are neither important nor implemented quickly, leave for the time being on the side. It is necessary to approach the pragmatic points. So it may be that a university degree significantly increased your chances, but in most cases will last too long. A revision of your resume, however, has not as much effect as the Dr. title, and can be accomplished relatively quickly for it.

TWO
Expand focus

Although it was for people two generations ago still common to spend their entire working life with the same employer, most workers today have worked in a variety of industries, positions and functions. In fact, a change of job is more accurately always a rewarding time to look at the labor market, and to gain an impression of the challenges that correspond with your own wishes and abilities.

Search areas and professional fields

To expand the search focus, there are totally different techniques. The best, most beneficial way for me is personally approaching brainstorming. This technique is designed to help you figure out respectively which sites come into your question for the bodies which they are suitable with your skills, knowledge and aptitudes.

Brainstorming approach

The brainstorming-approach is about coming out to be quite frank. Take four large leaves at hand. On the first you write largely the words "Experience," on the second "free time", the third "talents" and the fourth "dream jobs".

Work experience

Make a note now in your journal "Experience", which is all the activities that you have ever done in your life. Do not forget any part-time jobs, summer jobs, temporary jobs, volunteer activities and everything in the broadest sense that could be an occupation (whether you have taken any money or not). If you maintain the rose garden of your elderly neighbor in your free time, then you should write that down also. Brainstorming lives when we set no limits for ourselves.

Free time

In the area of leisure write down all the activities that you perform in your spare time or which you are concerned with. These include hobbies, activities in associations and the issues upon which you educate yourself in your free time. If you work intensively with cacti, read a lot about it and how to maintain it, then this information belongs on this sheet.

Talents

Are there things that you are really good at? If you do not have any ideas for this topic, ask people who know you well.

Dream jobs

Have you always dreamed of exploring the Amazon jungle as a researcher, or as a fireman to stop fires or to be hired as an astronaut at NASA? Here is the place to record it.

Browsing-approach

An alternative approach is to extend the search focus is the browsing approach. To do this, depending on a branch and a list of vocational fields, use the internet to find them. Of course you can leave out industries and career fields where you do not want to work with. All the others should be written in the first column of a table. In the second column you can complete experiences, competencies and qualifications in this sector (resp. This career field) either demanded or at least helpful, and which you are able to cover.

For industries and professional fields which you do not have any experience, skills or qualifications in, you can discard. For all others, it benefits you to take a closer look and use the analysis called the Interface-diagram-approach.

Supply-Chain-Approach

The supply chain approach is the third technique for expanding your search area. It is based on a closer examination of the value chain.

Start from a certain activity that the "adjacent" functional areas are analyzed. This approach is based on the following consideration: There is a relatively high probability that someone who has worked in a certain area also has some experience in related fields. So it is conceivable that an employee of a spare part procurement also has a certain idea about inventory accounting or that someone from the sales department has some idea about marketing, especially positions and responsibilities that are spread widely in the company.

There is also the possibility that over delegates in adjacent areas, additional and not conscious competencies were built. Likewise, a few skills along the supply chain of several people must be controlled. For example, the manufacturers of fast-food products hygiene regulations in the food industry should be known by the chef or the staff which specializes in a Catering and Cleaning Company.

Upstream activities

Under upstream activities you understand the activities that must be completed before you perform your actual work. Just as the vegetables must harvested, sold, be bought and cleaned before the cook can prepare a delicious dish from it.

Downstream activities

This includes activities that are pending after you have done your job. Using the Chef example, the waiter has brought the plate with your vegetables to the table, and later clears empty plates. Subsequently, the plates and cutlery are washed, remnants discarded and the table is newly covered after the departure of the guest.

Side bearing activities

These activities are closely related with your activity, but were done at the same time as you did your work - only without depending on you. For example, parallel to you is a sommelier (or wine consultant), who has recommended the guests wines that harmonize perfectly with the chosen meal. Perhaps there was in your kitchen, a division of labor and while you have processed vegetables, a grill master has roasted noble meat.

Also check whether your operation took place outside activities which extend the value chain in parallel to yours. Some might have vegetables processed by the same provider at a manufacturer of fast-food products, a food technologist. Such issues should be especially considered if they have a high affinity to your experiences.

Interface-diagram-approach

The interfaces-diagram-exam is a wonderful opportunity to verify found ideas. Draw this onto the largest possible paper, with three overlapping circles with the titles: "What I can," "What I want" and "what is required"??

- What I can?
- What I want?
- What is required?

Make a note now for every idea found in a separate diagram. Ideally, the areas of what you want, what you can do and what is required should largely overlap. But it will hardly be a wholly-owned overlap. Let yourself not be discouraged. When the areas of mutual overlap is very small, you should check this particular professional idea again or build the necessary competencies.

THREE

Define your customizable targeted offer

Ideally, you will find a handful of other professional ideas from the chapter entitled "Focus". There are also those activities which have been carried out successfully and those that you would like to exercise again. The task now is to create individual offers for the different areas (or even individual employers).

It's not about you inventing some sort of lie, but that you create from your profile with your experience, your knowledge and your skills those subjects to the fore, which are for a potential employer in the said area important.

Self marketing

"The bait has to be tasty to the fish, not the fisherman," is a conventional wisdom. Geared for the subject of job search, this means that self-marketing presupposes that one is dealing with the needs of those company where you want to work. The AIDA approach and knowledge of your personal USPs are two important aspects in the development of a marketing strategy, whether it is about a new variety of pasta, a luxury car or your job performance.

AIDA-Approach

One does not speak at random about an application. Of course, with every sincere application comes the fact that you offer a prospective employer your job performance. But a successful approach from the business community is the AIDA principle. Firstly, it will have to attract the (attention) of a customer by awakening the customers (interest), then it has to suggest that it is able to fufill the (desire) of the customer, in order to induce him to finally take (action). The desired action is in our case, that it invites employers to attend an interview.

Attention

You must ensure that you stand out from the pile of resumes in the post, the mailbox or the online application tool in a positive way. Just so you get the recipient to have a look at your records accurately. Instruments for this could be a special attractive design, professional photography, or an unexpected response. In any case, observe that the attention should go hand in hand with a positive feeling about this. Who stands out negatively, will not increase his chances in the normal case.

Interest

Interest arises when your profile (mostly) matches with the need of the employer and additionally convinces with professionalism and credibility. This happens when the described facts and arguments are understandable. It is also important for many recruiters to "feel" the person behind the profile. A good set of application documents is in any case has "personality".

Desire

Who looks through application documents for a particular location, is located in the most about the same. Candidates who apply in German and English for a job as a clerk, will in most cases have comparable training, work experience and language skills in comparison to their competition. Behind similar applications are often very different people with different fates, experience, skills and designs. These are barely visible at a rapid screening of documents.

At this stage you have already attracted the attention, and your documents have also been found interesting. Now it comes the time to trigger the impression of the recruiter that you are exactly the right person for the advertised job and he should invite you for an interview.

Action

It is always surprising how hard candidates make it to get in contact with them for an interview. Often the phone number is incorrect and e-mail boxes are full. It also happens that the outgoing messages end up in voice boxes and telephone responders, giving a good impression to the possible employer for the opposite conclusion, that is that the candidate has built up not a lot of effort. Check very carefully to see if your contact details are accurate, and provide ample free space in your mailboxes for replies and announcements, for it corresponds to the impression you want to give your potential employer.

Your USP (unique selling proposition)

The outstanding future is called as the unique selling proposition (or unique selling point, USP), with which an offer clearly stands out from the competition in the marketing and sales psychology. Synonym is veritable client advantage. The unique selling point should be "defensible", oriantated at targeted groups and economics and are achieved in price, time and quality. The concept is part of the basic vocabulary of marketing. A unique feature, ie a unique value proposition is to be connected to the product.

Source: Wikipedia

In an application, your performance comes to mediate a potential employer as positive as possible. Note, however, that the perception of what is a USP depends on the audience. In the perspective of a company, it can be a huge advantage if you know a machine so well after many years that you can weigh and repair itself. For another company which does not use said machine, the evidence may be reduced to: "has a certain technical skills and practical experience." A successful application strategy - especially for people with some professional experience - leads away from mass broadcast and towards a very targeted customer approach, where applications and location can be tailored individually as well as to each other.

If you work at it, work out your USP for a specific position, you should also think about this: a USP should be a unique, motivating and verifiable value proposition. Any verbal bubbles are just as out of place as self praise.

Helpful questions in connection with the drafting of your USP can be:

- Why should the company just you hire and not your competitors?
- What do you have to offer the company which is valuable for this and what can only you offer?

Always answer these questions from the perspective of your potential employer.

It is possible that your UPS is not in a single ability or experience, but in the combination of several skills. It is this mix that makes you unique. However, you should not overuse the uniqueness theme. You need not be the only person on the planet who has to make a specific offer. It is enough altogether if you are the only one with said UPS who applies at the company and is available for the company as a potential employee.

FOUR
Conclusion

If you have worked through the steps of this guide with your own profile (only reading barely helps you to go further), you should now be able to formulate a clear profile to prospective employers.

Whether you thereby receive more invitations to interviews is highly dependent on your profile and the desired area. But what I can say from my own experience as a recruiter is that you will get a lot of targeted invitations. The more accurate your potential employer perceives you in advance, the more likely it is that the place to which you have applied will bring you closer to getting employed.

Disclaimer

Introduction

By using this book, you accept this disclaimer in full.

No advice

The book contains information. The information is not advice and should not be treated as such.

No representations or warranties

To the maximum extent permitted by applicable law and subject to section below, we exclude all representations, warranties, undertakings and guarantees relating to the book.

Without prejudice to the generality of the foregoing paragraph, we do not represent, warrant, undertake or guarantee:

- that the information in the book is correct, accurate, complete or non-misleading.

- that the use of the guidance in the book will lead to any particular outcome or result.

Limitations and exclusions of liability

The limitations and exclusions of liability set out in this section and elsewhere in this disclaimer: are subject to section 6 below; and govern all liabilities arising under the disclaimer or in relation to the book, including liabilities arising in contract, in tort (including negligence) and for breach of statutory duty.

We will not be liable to you in respect of any losses arising out of any event or events beyond our reasonable control.

DISCLAIMER

We will not be liable to you in respect of any business losses, including without limitation loss of or damage to profits, income, revenue, use, production, anticipated savings, business, contracts, commercial opportunities or goodwill.

We will not be liable to you in respect of any loss or corruption of any data, database or software.

We will not be liable to you in respect of any special, indirect or consequential loss or damage.

Exceptions

Nothing in this disclaimer shall: limit or exclude our liability for death or personal injury resulting from negligence; limit or exclude our liability for fraud or fraudulent misrepresentation; limit any of our liabilities in any way that is not permitted under applicable law; or exclude any of our liabilities that may not be excluded under applicable law.

Severability

If a section of this disclaimer is determined by any court or other competent authority to be unlawful and/or unenforceable, the other sections of this disclaimer continue in effect.

If any unlawful and/or unenforceable section would be lawful or enforceable if part of it were deleted, that part will be deemed to be deleted, and the rest of the section will continue in effect.

Law and jurisdiction

This disclaimer will be governed by and construed in accordance with Swiss law, and any disputes relating to this disclaimer will be subject to the exclusive jurisdiction of the courts of Switzerland.

www.ingramcontent.com/pod-product-compliance
Lightning Source LLC
Chambersburg PA
CBHW020716180526
45163CB00008B/3109